Nature in Action
GROWING UP

by Oxford Scientific Films

Written by Jill Bailey M S

P9-DTL-983

MAYFLOWER BOOKS
NEW YORK

About this book

What does a newborn mouse look like? How does a giant redwood tree start life? Throughout nature, living creatures are constantly growing and changing – in different ways and for different reasons. Some life stories are familiar: we all know that birds lay eggs. But how many eggs are laid, and how long do they take to hatch? Not all animals' eggs hatch into miniature adults – the young of many creatures are very different from their parents. A caterpillar leads quite a different life from its butterfly parent; and many shellfish living on the sea floor have young that swim in the surface waters of the oceans, tiny strange shapes like creatures from another world. Even fish eggs do not always hatch into miniature versions of their parents.

Many animals produce thousands or even millions of offspring in a lifetime, yet the world does not become overcrowded. Young animals and plants provide an easy source of food for other animals, and over the years creatures have developed a variety of ways of protecting their young and giving them a better chance of survival. This is not just a display of parental feelings –.it is in the animals' own interest that their young live to become adults: the more babies that survive, the fewer need be produced to replace their parents, and the less time and energy need be spent in the business of reproduction.

The degree to which parent animals take an interest in their offspring varies greatly. Some fish actually eat their young if they get the chance, while others devotedly guard their eggs and young. Some baby animals get their food in the form of egg yolk. Mammals protect their young inside their own bodies until they are well-developed, supplying them with food from their own blood and after birth feeding them on milk. Plants pack their seeds with stored food to give the young seedling a good start in life.

The complex stages of development from egg to adult, the hazards faced by young plants and animals, and the many ways in which they cope with them are all part of the fascinating study of growing up.

The spotted coat of a four-day-old white-tail deer blends with the sunlight dappling the floor of the forest. It sits perfectly still so as not to attract the attention of enemies while waiting for its mother to return.

All shapes and sizes

Every living creature grows at some time in its life. But what exactly is growth? What is the difference between an animal or plant growing up and a balloon being blown up? Both get bigger. But the balloon's 'growth' is only temporary – sooner or later it loses air and shrinks, and it may be blown up and let down several times during its 'life'. For living creatures, growth is a permanent increase in size, caused by the creation of new living matter.

Nor is growth simply an increase in size or weight. For most creatures, getting bigger also involves becoming more complicated. The new living matter is formed into organs (body structures) and tissues for doing special jobs – moving the muscles, circulating the blood, powering the brain and so on. In many animals and plants the organs which carry out reproduction are not developed until the animal or plant reaches a certain size or age. This development of specialized structures is called 'differentiation' – the making of differences.

Coiled, springy tendrils help the passion flower to climb up other plants, to reach the light.

For many animals, growth continues slowly throughout much of their lives, slowing down or stopping only when a certain size and complexity has been reached. Young animals usually grow at a faster rate than older ones: a baby will more than double in weight in the first year of its life. For insects, which have a hard outer covering, for shelled animals such as crabs, and for animals with tough scaly skins such as snakes, growth happens in a series of short bursts. The shell or skin is shed at intervals, and the animal then grows rapidly while the new coat is still soft enough to stretch. Once it has hardened, it prevents growth until the next 'molt' of shell or skin.

A coat for each season

There can be other reasons for molting. Animals living in regions where there are hot

5

and cold seasons grow thick fur in winter, then shed it in summer. Some animals which rely on camouflage for protection shed their coat every spring and autumn. For example, arctic hares have brown fur in summer to match the moorland, then shed it in autumn and grow a white coat to match the winter snows. Even trees may shed their leaves in winter to avoid losing water by evaporation from the leaves at a time when the ground is too frozen for the roots to take up water.

A mother hippopotamus has only one baby at a time, and she looks after it very carefully.

Insects as big as elephants?

The pattern of growth of any living creature depends upon its size and shape. Why do insects never grow to be as big as elephants? Animals grow in different ways according to the way they are built. The irregular growth of insects and shelled animals might appear to be a disadvantage, but having a skeleton outside the body (an 'exoskeleton') instead of inside (an 'endoskeleton') has a lot of advantages. Exoskeletons are usually light and strong, and all the body tissues are protected by them. Exoskeletons also help to prevent the animals' bodies from drying out.

However, once an animal reaches a certain size, an exoskeleton becomes unsuitable. It would be so large that the total weight would be unbearable. Also, when molting, the animal would collapse under the weight of its own tissues before the new skeleton had hardened. So larger animals have internal bony skeletons instead, rather like the girders of a building. Only the most delicate body structures, such as the brain and the spinal cord, are completely protected by bone.

Plants overcome the problem of size by producing woody supports. Plants have a very different pattern of growth from animals. Most animals' tissues continue growing throughout life; but in plants, growth occurs only in certain special parts. Only the tips of the shoots and roots can grow. Here, the cells (tiny units of living matter) multiply, then swell by taking in water, and finally 'differentiate' – become specialized to perform various tasks. Once a plant cell has differentiated it can no longer divide. These cells divide only in the spring and summer, when there is a good supply of food and water for growth. So growth in plants is a seasonal process.

Because plants need light to make their food,

their growth is affected by the amount of light they get and the direction from which it comes. It is an advantage for a plant to grow tall so that it is not shaded by other plants. Some plants make use of others to help them reach the light. Instead of using valuable energy and food making woody tissues for support, they climb up other plants. Ivy clings to tree trunks with little suckerlike roots. Beans twine their stems around any available support, while peas have some of their leaves changed into tendrils (twisting green tentacles) for climbing. Stem-twining plants are remarkable in that they always turn the same way – hops always wind themselves clockwise around a support, convolvulus ('bindweed') counterclockwise.

Looking for light

Developing leaves twist their stalks to take up positions where they will receive most light. Anyone who lies on the floor of a woodland and looks up at the branches above will see that very few leaves overlap. This carefully arranged pattern is called a 'leaf mosaic'. Some plants bend towards light: the side away from the light grows faster than the side nearest the light. Houseplants on windowsills often bend in this way.

The effects of gravity

The roots of a plant grow towards the center of the earth under the influence of gravity. If a young seedling is placed on its side, its roots will bend to grow down into the soil again, and the shoots will bend upwards away from the soil. Spacing of plants is also governed by the food and water supply for growth, since plants cannot move. Desert plants usually grow scattered at regular intervals, the spacing being a measure of the amount of soil each needs to get enough food and water.

Two young starfish (top) shelter beside a larger one. Starfish can grow new bodies from their broken-off limbs.
When the hermit crab (middle) grows too big for his borrowed home, a cast-off seashell, he will find a new one to move into.
Autumn leaves (left) show a mosaic pattern designed to catch as much light as possible.

From egg to chick

Nobody knows which came first – the chicken or the egg. But at least the growth of a chick until its moment of birth can be followed from the very beginning. Eggs are made in special parts of the mother chicken. When the eggs are ready to be laid they pass down a long winding tunnel (the 'oviduct') to the outside. During this journey a number of interesting changes take place.

When first formed, each egg is made up of just one cell – a single tiny unit of living matter – containing instructions from both the mother and the father (the hen and the rooster) on how to develop into a new chicken. This cell will multiply again and again to produce all the cells of the new chick's body. As soon as it starts to multiply, it is called an 'embryo'. As the egg passes down the oviduct, various layers are built up around it. First is the yolk, a bright yellow ball which provides food for the developing embryo. (The exact color of the yolk depends upon what the hen was eating before she produced the egg.) The yolk is contained within a thin, transparent skin. Around the yolk is the clear, jelly-like substance – the 'white' of the egg. This contains more food for the embryo, as well as supplying it with water. This layer is also surrounded by a skin, and at the wide end of the egg there is an air space between the 'white' and the eggshell. The developing embryo needs to breathe, and this space contains an air supply, which can be kept up by air seeping in through tiny holes in the shell. The shell is the last layer to be added, and once it has hardened the egg is ready to be laid.

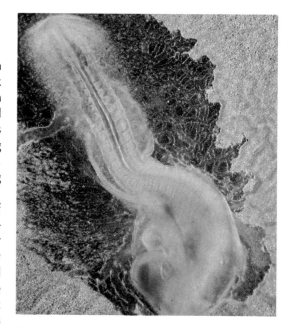

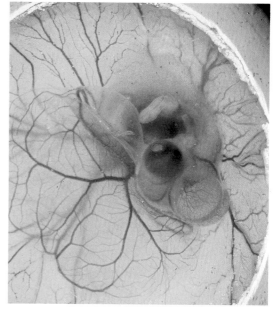

Warm and safe

Usually birds lay their eggs in carefully prepared, warmly lined nests well hidden and protected from enemies. If it is to develop, an egg must be kept warm; so one of the parents (usually the mother) 'broods' it by covering it with her body. She will probably have special 'brooding patches' on her breast – areas without feathers where the egg can come directly

8

into contact with the warm skin. While she is brooding she will be fed by her mate. Some birds take it in turns to brood their eggs. They may start as soon as the first egg is laid, in which case some chicks will hatch sooner than others; or they may wait a few days until all the eggs have been laid.

During this brooding period the egg begins to develop. The first cell multiplies to form two

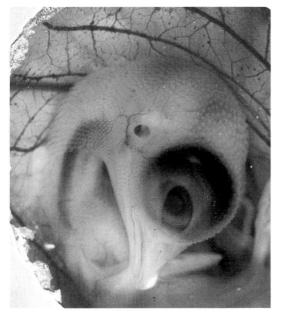

In a two-day-old chick embryo (opposite left) the eyes are already developing.
A five-day-old chick embryo (opposite below), firmly connected to the surrounding yolk, has quite a well-developed head.
At nine days, the chick embryo (left) begins to look more like a bird.
At last the chick (below left) breaks out of its shell, still wet from the fluid that cushioned it.

In a newly laid egg the embryo can hardly be seen – a mere black speck tucked away at one side of the yolk. It is difficult to imagine that eventually this little speck will grow to fill the whole egg. How is such a tiny creature ever going to use its enormous food supply? While the chick embryo is developing, a network of tiny blood vessels spreads out over the yolk and along the edge of the air space. The blood absorbs food from the yolk and air from the air space and carries them back to the embryo. Because its lungs are not yet properly developed, the embryo uses air dissolved in the blood. Later, it will breathe air directly from the air space.

Gradually the yolk and white are used up, and the developing chick comes to fill the space they once occupied. Its limbs and beak develop and it becomes covered in a coat of soft, fluffy down. Once it has made its way into the cold world outside the egg, this down will keep it warm until it acquires a layer of fat to keep the cold out. Then it will grow stiff, oily feathers like those of its parents.

Breaking out

When it is ready to hatch, the chick starts cheeping inside the egg. This attracts the attention of its mother, who calls to it. Encouraged by this, and helped by a special 'tooth' at the end of its beak, the chick pecks its way out of the egg, emerging bedraggled and wet from the remains of the egg white. Soon it dries out, and its down looks like a fluffy yellow ball. Its egg tooth is shed now that it is no longer needed. The chick is able to run around almost immediately but needs to learn from its mother what makes good food and what does not. At first it will peck at any likely looking objects on the ground.

cells, then these also multiply, and so on to form the new chick. As they multiply, different groups of cells develop into different structures. At quite an early stage the chick's backbone can be seen, and the head with its eyes. Gradually the head becomes more complicated, with large eyes, a brain and the beginnings of a beak, and from the backbone the limbs start to develop as small bumps.

First days of a plant

Seeds are to plants what eggs are to birds, and in some ways seeds and eggs are very similar. Just as the chicken's egg contains an embryo chick, so a seed contains an embryo plant surrounded by food tissues and protected by a tough outer coat. The embryo is formed from a plant egg that has been fertilized by a pollen grain.

The food in a seed is usually stored in one of two ways. In a corn seed (the kernel), for example, near the scar where the seed was joined to the 'cob' there is a tiny plant embryo, with minute pointed root and shoot. The rest of the seed is a tissue full of stored food, formed while the seed was still attached to its parent. The developing embryo absorbs its food from this tissue. The way food is stored inside a lima bean, on the other hand, is quite different. Inside the seed coat is a tiny embryo plant, whose first two leaves – the 'cotyledons' or seed leaves – have become swollen with food. The tiny shoot is tucked away between these two thick leaves.

Unlike a bird's egg, a seed may wait several years before it develops into a plant. Sooner or later a seed gets into the soil: maybe just by

A tiny root (above) pushes out through the coat of a germinating sycamore seed. The wing on the fruit shows that it is carried by the wind away from the parent tree.

falling from the parent plant, or by being blown, washed along by rain, or deposited in the waste of the animal that ate the fruit containing the seed. Here, protected from the weather, the seed waits until conditions are good enough for it to grow. A young seedling is delicate and easily damaged by frost, so the seed waits for a suitable temperature. It also needs oxygen from the air in the soil to help it burn up its stored food to produce energy for growth. Seeds usually have very dry tissues, so, when it starts to grow, a seed must first take up water. Some of its stored food must be used to make new plant tissues, and the seed needs water in which to dissolve this stored food so that it can be moved to the growing shoot and root. Water is also needed for the newly formed cells to expand.

At some point in the seed coat is a little hole – the 'micropyle' – through which water can enter. Because it needs so much water, the first

part of the seedling to emerge from the seed coat is the root. This grows down into the soil under the influence of gravity, and on its surface it develops many root hairs which increase the surface area of the root for absorbing water. The tip of the root is covered with a cap of loose slimy cells, which protects the delicate growing point as it pushes down through the soil, and helps to lubricate the passage of the root.

Growing and changing

The stem of a little bean shoot pushes up, bent over like a hook, through the soil. When it emerges into the light it straightens up, pulling the newly developing leaves above the ground. As the little shoot and root develop, some cells differentiate (become specialized) to form a system of tubes carrying water up from the root to the shoot and food down from the shoot to the root. As the stored food is used up the cotyledons shrivel away. Plants make their food by using the green pigment in the leaves to trap the energy of sunlight. As the young leaves expand the seedling starts to make its own food, and soon it can do without its stored food.

How to stay upright

The young seedling is at first supported by the pressure of water in its tissues. A plant cell is surrounded by an elastic wall, and as the cell takes up water this wall stretches until it can stretch no more. The cell is then stiff, rather like a bicycle tire pumped full of air. As the plant grows bigger, this support is not enough. The cells of the plant's water-carrying system are woody and provide some support but large plants, such as trees and shrubs, need more – they must get thicker as they grow taller. In order to do this, trees have two rings of special dividing cells in their stems. One, around the middle of the stem, produces extra woody tissue for carrying water and minerals to the growing crown of branches and extra tubes for taking food to the roots. The other ring of dividing cells is near the outside of the stem, producing more stem tissue and a protective layer of 'bark' on the outside.

An oak seedling (top) is using up the food stored in the acorn to make a root and shoot. Sycamore seedlings (above) push through the carpet of last autumn's dead leaves on the woodland floor, to reach the light.

The fantastic water babies

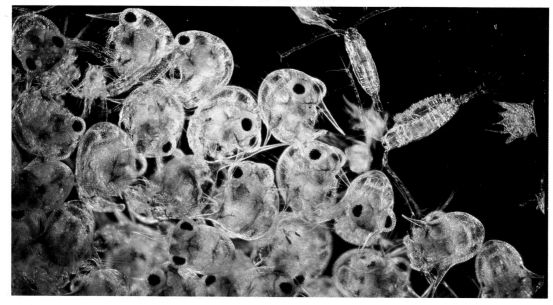

The layers of water near the surface of the sea usually appear to be almost empty of living creatures. But in fact this water is teeming with tiny animals and plants, known together as 'plankton', which are mostly too small to be seen with the naked eye. Under a microscope this wonderland can be explored, and it can be seen that most of the billions of planktonic creatures are really the babies of much larger, quite familiar animals. In fact the plankton is rather like an enormous mixed-up nursery of young creatures, all growing up in different ways.

Even through a microscope, however, it is often impossible to recognize what kind of animal one of these planktonic creatures will turn out to be. When they first hatch out from the underwater egg masses, they are quite unlike their parents in shape or size and often look like fantastic creatures from outer space. They change their form at least once, and often several times, before they become adults. Each distinct change in form is called a 'metamorphosis'.

Changing shape

In the sea and on the seashore there are millions of animals with hard outer shells,

Tiny crab larvae (above) settle on the sea bed, where they will gradually develop into adult crabs.

instead of internal skeletons. They include crabs, lobsters, barnacles, shrimps, and prawns. Most of them hatch from the egg as young creatures quite unlike the adult form and are known as 'larvae'. Some may pass through ten different larval stages before becoming adults. For instance, crab eggs hatch into small spiny larvae, which swim among the plankton (tiny floating plants and animals of the surface waters of oceans and lakes). After several molts and slow changes in form, they develop into larger larvae which look a little more like their parents and can walk as well as swim. Finally, as they get bigger and heavier, they drift down from the surface water layers containing plankton to start life as bottom-living crabs.

Most of the larval forms of marine creatures are delicate and transparent (making them almost invisible to predators) and live among the plankton, usually feeding on the tiny planktonic plants. They can swim using many small whip-like hairs called 'cilia'. Eventually the growing larvae become too heavy to swim in this way and descend to the sea bottom. When they 'settle out' to live on the sea bed, they

often make a big change in their choice of food, starting, as soon as they are big enough, to eat other animals.

Some sea animals, such as the barnacles that encrust rocks and even the bottom of ships, stay in one spot for all their adult lives, but their young have much more freedom, being able to swim.

The shapes taken by planktonic young are often very strange and also beautiful. Starfish larvae are very attractive with their slender, curved arms. Jellyfish larvae can look like flowers, with their array of tiny petal-like tentacles, and their delicate colors. Sea snail larvae swim with the aid of little 'wings' which they jerk and flap to keep on the move.

Considering the many large animals that live on plankton—from the adults of the planktonic creatures themselves to fish and even gigantic whales – it is rather a surprise that any of these tiny babies ever survive to go through all their metamorphoses and become adults. But when they do grow up, their eggs are produced in such huge numbers that enough young survive, and the balance of life in the sea is maintained.

Part of the chain of millions of eggs (top left) laid by a single sea snail.
No, it's not a monster from outer space (left): it's just a tiny lobster larva.
It looks like a flower (below), but this larva will eventually turn into a jellyfish.

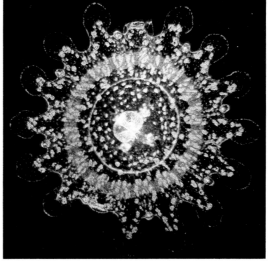

Amazing insects

Sea creatures are not the only animals whose young go through several changes of shape, or 'metamorphoses', on their way to adult life. Many insects go through similar changes, and their different life stages are often a familiar sight in homes, gardens and the countryside.

An adult insect almost always lays her eggs on the kind of food that the young will need. Beetles may lay eggs in tunnels in tree bark, butterflies lay them on the leaves of food plants, and flies lay them on the bodies of dead animals. Mosquitoes float them in raft-like bundles on the surface of ponds, while stick insects simply drop them like a rain of small bullets from the leaves. The lacewing mother tries to prevent her cannibal young from eating each other by attaching each egg separately to a leaf by a long slender stalk.

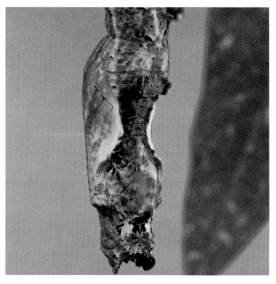

Inside each egg an insect embryo develops, absorbing the yolk and becoming a small grub or 'larva'. When it is ready to hatch, the larva either eats its way out of the egg or produces chemicals which dissolve away the egg case. Larvae take many forms, ranging from the caterpillars of butterflies and moths to the maggots of flies and the underwater dragonfly 'nymphs'.

As soon as it leaves its egg, the young larva starts to feed, eating almost nonstop until it is ready to change into an adult. It often does not eat the same food as its parent or even live in the same kind of surroundings. A butterfly, for example, sips nectar from flowers, while its caterpillar crunches its way through green leaves. The dragonfly hovers on its transparent wings in the air, while its larva lives underwater in ponds and rivers.

During this stage the insect larva has to grow as a result of all the food it is eating. Usually it grows by shedding its skin or 'molting': the old skin splits and the larva comes out in a new, soft skin which can stretch before it finally hardens.

At a certain size or age the larva stops eating and prepares to undergo another change of form. It sheds its skin for the last time and turns into a 'pupa', an immovable hard shell often wrapped in a fluffy cocoon of silk to protect it.

The story of the Gulf Fritillary butterfly starts with the egg (top left), laid on passion flower leaves. From it hatches the hungry caterpillar (bottom left). Later, the caterpillar becomes a pupa (middle left) in which its body changes completely. Finally the adult butterfly (below) emerges and rests while its crumpled wings expand and dry.

Inside the apparently sleeping pupa a miraculous change takes place. The larva body is rearranged into a completely new pattern: it forms the legs, wings, and internal organs that it will need as an adult insect. When this is completed, the skin of the pupa splits and the adult insect pulls itself out. At first its wings are crumpled and folded, but as blood is pumped into them they expand and finally harden and dry. After a while the brand-new insect takes to the air and starts its adult life.

Not all insects pass through all these stages. Some, like the locusts, crickets and grasshoppers, hatch from the egg as miniature adults, usually lacking wings, and with each successive molt they become more like the adult insect.

The butterfly's tale

The development of the Gulf fritillary butterfly, shown on these pages, is typical of butterflies, moths and many other insects. Eggs are laid on the leaves of passion flowers. After a few days the tiny caterpillar eats its way out of the egg case, then proceeds to eat the rest of the case, which forms a nourishing food. Then it starts to eat the passion flower leaves, biting off pieces with its sharp mouthparts, using its stumpy legs and sucker-like feet to cling to its food. The caterpillar's bright colors probably serve as a warning to predators. Its spines ooze a milky liquid which smells of vanilla and appears to be distasteful to other animals. The predators will remember that orange and black caterpillars are not good to eat.

When it reaches a certain size, the caterpillar stops eating and wanders off to one of the twining tendrils of the passion flower. Here it spins a little pad of silk, then hooks its tail end into the silk to dangle head-down from the tendril. It remains motionless for several weeks, while its skin darkens then hardens to form a shell around it. It is now called a 'pupa'. When the miracle of metamorphosis is complete, the adult butterfly breaks out of the pupal case. Then it rests, clinging to the old case, while its crumpled wings expand as the blood is pumped through them, and soon a new Gulf fritillary is ready to take to the air.

The frog fairy tale

In the popular fairy tale, a frog changes into a handsome prince. In real life, once a frog has become a frog, it does not change any more – but it has already undergone changes nearly as magical as turning into a prince!

Frogs (like toads, newts and salamanders) are among those animals known as amphibians, which spend part or all of their life in water but return to water to mate and lay their eggs. Each egg is coated with a jelly that quickly swells on contact with the water, making the eggs stick together to form masses of 'frog spawn'. Within a few days the egg – a black blob inside the jelly – takes on a definite shape, with a head and tail. After about ten days the tadpole hatches and attaches itself to a plant. At this stage it is still living off the food in the yolk – its mouth is not yet properly formed for eating.

The young tadpole has a round body with a long, ribbon-like tail, which it uses for swimming. It uses 'gills' to breathe air dissolved in the water. The gills are delicate frilly outgrowths on its head, well supplied with blood to carry the oxygen to the rest of the tadpole's body. These finger-like structures have a large surface area for absorbing dissolved oxygen.

After a few days the mouth opens and the

Frog spawn (below left) is a mass of frog's eggs. Very young tadpoles (above) have frilly external gills through which to breathe.
A tiny frog (above right) considers making his first trip on to land. The younger tadpole on his left has yet to develop his legs.
The marsupial frog (below) carries its eggs in a pouch on its back until they hatch.

tadpole begins to feed on microscopic plants which it scrapes from the surface of pond weeds with its horny toothed lips. During the next few weeks the tadpole grows rapidly, and eventually internal gills are formed – slits connecting the mouth with the outside, protected by a fold of skin, the 'operculum'. As it grows its diet changes: it starts to eat dead animals.

Coming up for air

About two months after hatching, the tadpole begins to develop lungs and comes to the surface frequently to gulp air. Where the tail joins the body, the hind legs begin to form, and later bud-like bumps bulge around the operculum indicating that the front legs, too, are starting to grow. The tadpole continues to swim like a fish, while the hind legs dangle beside its body.

Eventually, about three months after hatching, it stops feeding and lives for a time off its tail, which is gradually absorbed; it now depends upon its growing legs and webbed feet for swimming. It sheds its skin and with it the horny jaws of the larva, revealing a much wider frog-like mouth. Finally the young frog climbs out of the pond on to the land and

learns to use its long tongue to catch insects.

Most frogs grow up in this way; but some eggs are laid in damp soil, pass the tadpole stage inside the egg, and hatch as tiny frogs. The midwife toad wraps her string of eggs around the legs of the father, who carries them around until they hatch into tadpoles, when he takes them to water. Some tree frogs, living in moist tropical jungles, lay their eggs on wet leaves. When they hatch, the young tadpoles are carried on their father's back and dipped in water occasionally to keep them damp.

Newts and salamanders, which look rather, like lizards but do not have scales, have a life story like that of frogs. Some salamanders may give birth to live young – the eggs develop, pass through the tadpole stage and change into tiny adults before being born.

A few amphibians, like Peter Pan, never grow up; they stop at one of the larval stages. The mudpuppy – a North American salamander – still has external gills, with only tiny lungs, and can reproduce at this stage. Axolotls (larval salamanders) also have external gills and can mate and reproduce without growing up to the adult stage of the tiger salamander.

Travels and dangers

From the rich man's caviar to the poor man's cod roe, it's all fish eggs. Fish are among the greatest egg producers in the world, for their eggs and young are eaten by many other creatures – including man. A female cod may produce as many as five million eggs in one spawning, of which perhaps only two will survive to breed. The largest numbers of eggs are produced by fish that live in the open oceans, where the young fish will face the greatest hazards. Fish that live in more protected waters, such as rivers and lakes, lay fewer eggs than their seafaring cousins. Some such fish may attempt to give their offspring a better chance of surviving by keeping their eggs inside their bodies until they hatch, or even by guarding the young fish – the 'fry' – after they have hatched.

Sharks, skates and dogfish lay their eggs in cases which are popularly known as 'mermaids' purses'. Many fish eggs contain oil droplets to help them float, so that the young fry hatch in the surface waters which are rich in plankton, providing an ample supply of food. Herring eggs, on the other hand, sink to the sea bottom, where they stick to stones and weeds and are less easily seen by predators. Fish like salmon and trout, that shed their eggs in fast-flowing streams, lay them in gravel beds for protection. Sticklebacks protect their eggs by making 'nests' of pieces of water plants glued together.

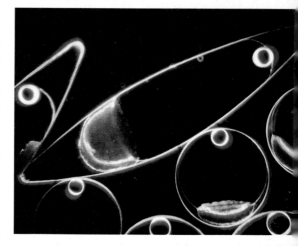

The amazing eels

Most fish eggs contain yolk, and the young fry hatch still attached to the yolk. They live by absorbing the yolk until their mouths are properly developed, when they are able to feed on tiny water plants and animals. This larval stage of fish may last as little as a few hours or as much as a few years – up to four years in the case of the sea lamprey. Like other underwater animals the larvae of fish are often very different from their parents. Freshwater eels have larvae which live in the sea and look rather like transparent leaves. When they were first discovered by scientists they were named as a new fish – a *Leptocephalus*. After a while the scientists noticed that these *Leptocephalus* fish were found only in certain parts of the Atlantic Ocean: tiny ones near the Sargasso Sea (a huge area of weedy water in the middle of the Atlantic) and larger ones in the Gulf Stream, the current of water that sweeps up to the coasts of Europe. But it was a long time before the amazing story of the eel was discovered. The adult eels, which live in fresh water, migrate from the rivers of Europe to the Sargasso Sea to spawn, and the *Leptocephalus* larvae ride the Gulf Stream back to Europe. During this journey, which may take several years, they gradually change into 'elvers' looking like miniature adult eels.

The salmon's pilgrimage

Another fish which also makes lengthy journeys

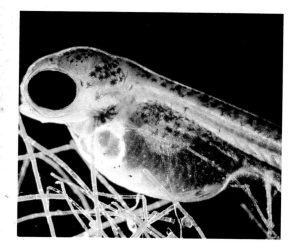

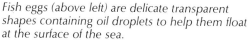

Fish eggs (above left) are delicate transparent shapes containing oil droplets to help them float at the surface of the sea.
Tiny fish embryos (below left) can be seen curled up inside these stickleback eggs.
A baby stickleback (above) still lives on the yolk stored in a sac on its belly.
The plaice (above right) looked very like a baby stickleback when it first hatched, but since then it has flattened and its face has twisted around to one side of its head.

between salt and fresh water is the Atlantic salmon, but it travels in the reverse direction to the eel. The eggs of the salmon hatch in mountain streams in Europe. The young grow through several larval stages during their two or three years in fresh water. Then they migrate as adults to the open ocean, finally returning over vast distances to mate and lay their eggs in the very same stream in which they were born.

How a flatfish gets flat

A surprising transformation happens during the development of young flatfish such as plaice and dabs. When it hatches a young flatfish looks very much like any other fish fry, with a rounded body, fins in the usual places, an eye on each side of the head and an 'air bladder' or bag of air inside its body to help it float. But soon its jaws start to twist sideways. During the next two to four months the fins along the back and underside grow along the whole length of the body. The body becomes thinner and flatter, until the fish can no longer swim in the

usual upright position: it has to lie on one side. Usually, what was the right side becomes the upper surface, and the left side becomes the lower surface. The young fish begins to swim on its side, rippling its body to propel itself. Most remarkable of all, the left eye moves around the head to lie alongside the right eye, so the fish ends up with two eyes beside each other, looking upwards. Only when this strange metamorphosis is complete does the young flatfish take to a new life on the bottom of the sea like its parents.

Escaping from danger

Most kinds of flatfish, such as plaice and turbot, have an extra method of protection from predators: not only are they colored to look like a stony sea bed, but they can change their color instantly to match new surroundings. Other fish larvae have special ways of protecting themselves from predators. Young herrings have a lot of jelly-like material in their muscles which makes them transparent and difficult to see. Haddock young can even hide among the tentacles of jellyfish, apparently unharmed by their stings.

Like the amphibian and insect larvae, young fish often have different feeding habits from their parents. Many fish that live as adults on the sea bottom have young that develop in the surface waters. Fish that eat other fish and small water animals may grow up feeding on tiny plants, until they are big enough and have strong enough jaws to hunt.

The scaly ones

Reptiles – snakes, lizards, crocodiles, tortoises, turtles – somehow give the impression of being tough and independent. It is hard to imagine a soft, helpless young reptile and, in fact, just as hard to find one. From the moment of their birth, reptiles must be strong enough to survive on their own.

Reptiles either lay eggs or give birth to live young which are exact miniatures of their parents. The eggs of reptiles are more complicated than those of their relatives, the amphibians. Because they are laid on land, they need support and protection, so they have tough leathery shells. This also helps to prevent the eggs from drying out in the air. Because the young must be very well developed by the time they hatch, reptile eggs contain plenty of yolk to nourish the developing embryo until it is strong enough to be born.

Reptile eggs are fertilized inside the female's body when she mates with a male. Like birds, she can store sperm (male sex cells) until her eggs are ready. Diamondback terrapins, for example, have been known to lay fertilized eggs four years after mating, and some snakes can store sperm for even longer periods.

A mother's club – of snakes

Those lizard-like reptiles, geckos and iguanas, usually lay only a single egg, while some snakes and turtles produce more than a hundred eggs at a time. Female grass snakes often gather together to lay their eggs, choosing a place where there is plenty of rotting plant material

When the garden lizard (above left) grows too big for his skin, he rubs it off and grows a new one. Bits of the old skin cling to the shiny new skin, making him look very untidy.
The female northern pine snake (right) lays a clutch of eggs with leathery white shells and coils around them to keep them warm and protect them until they hatch. The baby snakes (above) break out of the shells using a special 'egg tooth' at the end of the snout.
The young green turtle (left) is at risk from the moment of his birth. He hatches out of an egg buried in the sand and must scrabble to the surface and make a dash for the sea, escaping the attacks of predatory crabs and seabirds on the way.

so that the heat given off as the leaves rot helps to incubate the eggs. Several thousand eggs may be found together in these communal 'nests'.

Most reptiles do not make elaborate preparations for egg laying. Often the eggs are laid in a shallow hole in the ground; but turtles may dig pits in the sand up to 70 cm (24 in) deep and 1 m (3 ft) wide, lay their eggs, then cover them over with sand to hide them. The female American alligator makes a large nest mound, 2 m (7 ft) across and 1 m (3 ft) high, of mud and rotting plants. She scoops out a hollow in the center, lays twenty to thirty eggs in it, then covers them with mud and plants. For the two to three months while the eggs are developing she guards them and may even water them during dry weather. Just before hatching the babies start to croak. This attracts their

mother's attention, and she scrapes the top from the nest to help them escape.

The Nile monitor uses a ready-made incubator, laying her eggs in a hole scraped in a termite nest. The termites repair the damage, so concealing the eggs, and the nest forms a warm protective incubator. Many egg-laying snakes, such as pythons and cobras, guard their eggs by curling around them. The parent snakes may become very aggressive at this time.

Many young reptiles have a special 'egg tooth', a tough sharp scale on the nose for breaking their way out of the hard-shelled eggs. The egg tooth is lost soon after hatching, as it is no longer needed. Some snakes hatch while the eggs are still inside their mother; the snakes are born as miniature adults from eggs which are never 'laid'. In this way the young are protected inside the mother until ready to become independent. This has enabled the European adder, for example, to live and breed inside the Arctic Circle where the climate is too cold for its eggs to hatch if laid on the ground. The young of some lizards hatch at the very moment the eggs are laid.

A matter of size

Young reptiles like snakes and lizards grow by shedding their tough scaly skins at intervals, since the skin cannot stretch very much. The old skin becomes dry and colorless. At last it splits, and the snake wriggles out with a shiny, brightly colored new skin, leaving the old one behind like the discarded skin of a fruit. Lizards may not be so tidy – they rub their old skin off in pieces and look very scruffy during the molt.

Young tortoises have a problem – they cannot shed their shells. When they hatch, their plates of shell are soft and overlap. As they grow, the plates come to lie side by side. A newborn giant tortoise, of the kind found on a few islands in the Pacific and Indian Oceans, is very small. Even at eighteen months it is no bigger than a man's fist. But it goes on growing and growing for forty years, by which time it may be more than 1 m (3 ft) long and weigh about a quarter of a ton. If a human baby grew at the same rate, it would end up as a man some 6 m (20 ft) in height!

Protective parents

Most of the simpler animals do not take much care of their young. They tend to lay vast numbers of eggs just on the chance that one or two of them will manage to survive. Animals that have fewer young, however, have to take more care of them to make sure that they grow up safely. This is the basis for all the different kinds of parental care that can be found in the animal world. Very young animals are much more likely than their parents to fall prey to enemies. They are not so strong: they cannot run so fast or see so well and they have yet to learn about life by day-to-day experience. Many animal parents give their offspring a better chance of survival simply by guarding them for a time after they are born or hatched.

One of the most common parental tasks is to leave a food supply for their hatching youngsters. Dung beetles work in pairs to roll a large ball of dung to a chosen site. Then they bury it in the soil. The eggs are laid in a pit in the dung ball and covered lightly with dung, to provide plenty of food for the grubs when they hatch. This is so successful that these beetles need lay only two to four eggs each season. Many parasitic wasps paralyze insects or grubs with their stings, then lay their eggs on them, so

Cuddly Alaskan brown bear twin cubs (above) take a break from play to have a drink of milk.
A male sea horse (above right) has a swollen belly containing his developing babies.
Mother scorpion (right) loads her youngsters on to her back to keep them safe.
Young penguins (below right) in a nursery group.

providing the young with a supply of living food. Other wasps lay their eggs in plants; the plants respond by producing a 'gall' – a large mass of tissue – around the intruders, so providing food for the young larvae.

Many creatures guard their eggs until they hatch. The female earwig gathers her eggs together in a heap in her underground chamber and licks them all in turn. This seems to be necessary if the eggs are to hatch. The newly hatched earwigs nestle under their mother until they have molted twice, then they ungratefully turn around and eat her before dispersing to live their own lives! Some centipedes also guard their eggs and young, and millipedes lay their eggs in a nest of earth and saliva, coiling themselves around it for protection. Scorpions are ferocious mothers, carrying their babies in a cluster on their backs, protected by the deadly sting.

Spiders protect their young in many ways. Some lay their eggs in silken cocoons which they carry around with them until they are ready to hatch. Even tarantulas become quite maternal, sitting on their cocoons like broody hens. The trapdoor spider keeps her cocoon in her burrow, and the young remain safely inside the burrow for several months after hatching. The diving spider keeps her young in a silken air-filled diving bell. Spiders must take care not to guard their young too long, or their hungry babies may find their mother a convenient source of food.

Fish can be some of the most devoted parents. Blennies lay their eggs in empty shells or old bottles, where the male guards them, fanning them with his fins to give them a good air supply. Some fish, like the 'mouthbreeder' cichlid, offer their eggs and young even greater protection – by keeping them in their mouths! They may keep up to 20,000 eggs or small fry in their mouths at a time, occasionally letting them out to feed but sucking them in again if danger threatens. During this time the parents do not feed – or they might accidentally swallow the family!

Fathers that give birth

It is not always the mother that looks after the young. The male pipefish has a pouch or groove on his belly, in which the female deposits her eggs. When the young fry hatch they are released but return to the pouch for protection. The father sea horse also carries his unborn family in a pouch, where they absorb food from his own blood supply. When the young are ready to be born he goes through a series of muscular spasms, shooting them out one at a time. Unfortunately he often forgets who his tiny babies are and is quite likely to gulp one up for dinner. This carelessness is quite common among fish.

The more complex or 'advanced' the young animal, the more time it must spend with its parent before being able to look after itself. Animals like deer, sheep, dogs, horses and so on must suckle milk from their mother while they learn, by watching her, how to find their own food.

At home in the nest

Almost all birds take pains to look after their eggs and young. Sometimes the female bird is the only parent to take an interest in the young; sometimes both parents incubate the eggs and feed the youngsters; and occasionally the roles are completely reversed. The color of a bird's feathers is a clue to its parental activity; if it is to sit on a nest undisturbed by predators, a bird needs to be camouflaged in drab brownish colors. If the male has brightly colored plumage and broods the eggs on the nest, he will be literally a sitting target for predators.

Most birds will build nests in which to incubate their eggs. Building material may be collected near the nest or brought from a considerable distance away. Usually there is an outer layer of coarse material – twigs, sticks, straw or mud – while the inner lining is softer, of hair, wool or feathers.

Neat nest builders

The weaver birds of Africa strip off plant fibers and tie them into knots as well as weaving them, while the tailorbird sews leaves together to form the framework for its nest. Swiftlets mix mud with spit to make their tiny nests, the source of the famous 'bird's-nest soup'. Adélie penguins, nesting in the wastes of Antarctica, make nests of stones to keep their eggs off the frozen ground.

Not all birds make nests. Owls nest in hollow trees or take over the old nests of other birds. The female hornbill seals herself and her brood into a hollow tree for protection, being fed by her mate through a small hole.

From eggs to nestlings

For the eggs to hatch, they must be kept warm. The parent 'incubates' them by sitting on them. Often the parent bird has a 'brood

patch', a patch of bare skin where the eggs can come directly into contact with the bird's body. Brush turkeys build large mounds of rotting vegetation and bury their eggs in them where the heat of the fermenting vegetation incubates them. But keeping the eggs warm is not the only problem. The Egyptian plover buries its eggs and chicks in the sand to keep them cool during the scorching heat of day in the desert and fetches water to sprinkle over them.

Young birds usually have a coat of soft down at first and are often kept warm by their parents until they have developed their adult feathers. They remain in the nest, being fed by the parents; young nestlings can eat their own weight of food each day. The loud cheeping made by the babies every time the parents return to the nest, together with the bright color inside their open beaks, stimulates the parents to feed them. The adult birds also clean the nest, removing waste. If a predator approaches, the parent bird may try to distract it and lure it away by fluttering as if it had an injury such as a broken wing.

The first flight

Learning to fly must be a nerve-racking experience for a young bird! Usually the parents nudge them out of the nest, where it is not far from the soft grassy ground in case of bumpy landings. But for seabirds that nest on narrow cliff ledges there are no practice flights. Guillemot chicks leap off the ledges and plummet down to the sea despite rapid wing beats. On hitting the water they call to their parents, who escort them out to sea, where they learn to fish. Moorhen chicks are unusually devoted to their parents – they may stay near the nest to help their parents look after the next generation, their young brothers and sisters!

There are also the scroungers. Cuckoos, honeyguides, whydahs and cowbirds lay their eggs in the nests of other birds. Their eggs are often the same color as those of the bird that is acting as an unwilling host. The cuckoo may remove eggs from the host bird's nest and substitute her own. Often the cuckoo chick stabs and kills its foster-brothers, or tips them out of the nest. Either way, it remains the sole occupant of the nest to claim the undivided attention of its foster parents.

A hungry bluetit family (far left) clamours for food when father appears at the nest.
A snowy egret (left) rests for a moment before going to catch more food for her young.
Mallard ducklings (below) must be able to swim from the time they hatch.

Life with mother

Man and mice have much in common. They are both mammals: that is, they feed their young on milk made in the mother's body – something that no other living creatures do. Man, mice and other mammals are also very successful at living – they can adapt to all kinds of conditions, survive cold, live for a long time, and produce many healthy young in their lifetimes. Why should it be that a single baby mammal has a better chance of growing up than one of a thousand babies produced by, for example, a fish?

This high survival rate of their young is one of the reasons for the great success of mammals. Fewer young are produced because more survive. The secret of this survival is the long 'gestation' period – the period of development of the young while still inside their mother. During this time the embryo is warm and protected from outside hazards. The gestation period can vary from three weeks in a house mouse to 22 months in an elephant; it depends upon how well developed the young must be at birth in order to survive. A young house mouse is born naked and blind and will stay protected in the nest for several weeks, whereas a baby elephant needs to be able to travel with the herd almost immediately.

Feeding before birth

Spending so long in its mother's womb – the special chamber in her body for developing young – means that the young mammal needs a good food supply. The lining of the womb is rich in blood vessels, and the embryo becomes linked to its mother's blood supply by a thick stalk joined to its belly. Through this blood system the mother supplies the embryo with food as long as it is in her body. The mammal embryo is cushioned in the womb inside a fluid-filled bag. It has no direct air supply but receives all the oxygen it needs through the mother's blood.

At a certain point the young are ready to live in the outside world, and so they are born: the mother's womb contracts to push them out through the elastic tube to the outside.

At birth the fluid-filled sac around the embryo bursts – this is why newborn mammals are wet – and it starts to use its lungs to breathe air. Almost immediately the young mammal starts to feed, sucking milk from its mother's nipples. Milk is a complete food for mammals, and the period for which a mammal is suckled (fed on its mother's milk) varies enormously – a few weeks in a guinea pig but six or seven months in whales. Mammals living in water – such as whales and dolphins – may have to compromise between suckling their young and allowing them to get to the air to breathe. To get around this problem, a mother dolphin squirts her milk into her infant's mouth so it gets a good dose between each trip to the surface every half minute. The coypu, a kind of huge rat, has nipples on the side of her body so the babies can feed and keep their heads above water to breathe, while she swims lying on her stomach.

Not all mammals follow this pattern of

A great gray kangaroo (far left) checks that her baby or 'joey' is safely in her pouch. There he has food, warmth, protection and free rides until he is old enough to manage alone.
The harvest mouse (below) looks after her young in a cozy nest woven between the corn stalks. The babies are born blind and hairless, but it is not long before the young (left) venture out into the wide world – which must seem very big and frightening at first!

development exactly. The 'marsupials' (primitive Australian mammals, like kangaroos and koalas, with pouches to hold their babies) start the same way, with the young beginning their development in their mother's womb. But there is no special womb lining of blood vessels to provide food, so after a relatively short time the young are born, still naked, blind and with few of their body organs fully developed. Amazingly, they find their way unaided to a pouch on their mother's tummy where, clinging to her nipples with their mouths, they feed on her milk.

The egg-laying mammals

Even more primitive than the marsupials are the few mammals that still lay eggs! Only two such 'living fossils' are known – the duck-billed platypus and the spiny anteater of Australia. The young, after hatching, are suckled by their mother, feeding on milk which trickles out from slits on her tummy. The female spiny ant-

eater grows a pouch during the breeding season, incubating the single egg in it and later suckling the youngster in there. The marsupials' pouch is a warm cozy shelter for their young and, not surprisingly, they may have difficulty persuading their offspring to leave it. Female kangaroos have been seen fighting off very large youngsters determined to return to the pouch!

A nursery for the babies

Other mammals may build nests in which to rear their young. Tree squirrels build several nests, known as 'dreys', of twigs, bark, leaves and moss, and use one of them as a nursery drey. Beavers have special nursery chambers in their lodges. Pack rats build stick houses of considerable height, protecting the entrances with hundreds of piled-up cactus spines. When the young are mature, the adult pack rats leave the house to the children and move out to build another for the next generation!

Childhood days

A baby mammal, with its soft fur and appealing uncertain manner, is seldom far from its mother. Because all young mammals need to feed on their mother's milk, they are bound to stay close to her until they are ready to feed themselves. For many young mammals, their mother is far more than a milk machine. The intelligence and skill of mammals in hunting and in avoiding being hunted are not fully developed at birth. Much is learned by experience, so the baby mammal needs to spend time in the company of adults.

In general animals which feed on plants (herbivores) are constantly at risk from the meat-eating animals (carnivores), so their young need to be ready to escape from enemies almost as soon as they are born. A giraffe can stand alone a few minutes after it is born and can run with its mother within two days. By the time it is two weeks old it can run even faster than its mother! Most grazing animals, such as caribou, antelopes and gazelles, are born in a relatively well-developed state.

By contrast the babies of the hunting animals – wolves, bears, lions – can be protected by their parents against enemies, so are born in a very helpless state, often blind, with little fur, and weak. The young hunter must spend a long time learning from parents before it is able to fend for itself.

Keeping up with mother can be difficult when you are tiny. Young anteaters and young apes ride jockey-style on their mothers' backs until they are quite big. Even walrus babies hitchhike, gripping their mothers' back with their flippers, although they can perfectly well swim alone. A young elephant can hardly climb up on its mother's back, so it makes up for it by holding on to its mother's tail with its trunk.

Some mammals cooperate to rear their young. When a female elephant leaves the main herd to give birth, she is accompanied by one or two other females – known as 'aunties' – who help with the birth and later help to protect the young elephant. In the sea, young dolphins also have aunties as well as a mother to seek out protection if danger threatens.

Mother elephant (opposite) keeps a watchful eye on her baby as they walk through the bush. Bengal tiger cubs (above) enjoy a splashy game. Their playful tussles are practice for adult life.

African Cape hunting dogs rear all their young in a communal burrow. All the females may nurse all the pups – not necessarily just their own. When the pack goes hunting, some females and a few males stay behind to guard the pups. When the hunters return, they disgorge food to feed the pups and their guards. Cousins can be as helpful as aunties: in a monkey group young females often tag on to mothers and babies, taking it in turns to hold and groom the infants. This means that, if something happens to the mother, there will always be a friend to look after her baby.

For the more intelligent mammals, play is an essential part of growing up. It is largely through play that they learn hunting skills, cunning, agility in escaping from other animals, and the basic principles of defense. The play of many hunting animals resembles mock chases and mock kills. Foxes train their cubs in speed and accuracy by holding food just out of reach,

then jerking it away. As the young grow older, they accompany their parents on hunting trips, learning the skills firsthand. Once their adult teeth are developed they will be able to kill for themselves. Cheetahs and lions may bring back their prey alive for the young to learn to kill.

Much play involves imitating adults – playing at being grown-up. This is how animals learn – by watching and imitating. Young bear cubs rolling over and over in mock battles are practicing for the real fights of adulthood and developing their muscles at the same time. A kitten pouncing on a ball of yarn is unconsciously rehearsing future attacks on mice and other small animals.

Time to leave home

Sooner or later, usually when the mother is ready to have another baby, it is time for the young mammal to fend for itself. It may decide to leave home itself, or it may be driven out by its parents. Often young males, on reaching maturity, are regarded by their fathers as rivals for their mothers' affections.

Learning about life

As they cling to their mother's chest, a young orang-utan seems to be telling his baby brother some exciting stories.

Monkeys and apes – the animals known as 'primates' – have always held a strong attraction for humans, as they are so similar to us. Besides needing to learn to feed itself and to defend itself, a young primate such as a baboon needs to learn how to live in a social group. Like other primates, baboons have well-defined 'rules of society' and social behavior. The young baboon must learn to behave in the right way if it is to continue to live in the group, just as a human child must learn 'manners' and the difference between right and wrong.

From its birth a young baboon is in constant touch with its mother, clinging to her or being carried by her as she moves about. Later it will ride on her back 'piggyback' style. She suckles it and grooms it, keeping it clean, and prevents it from straying too far away by pulling it back by its tail. Baboons have a complex communication system of calls and gestures, which the young soon learn, running to their mother if called. This is important in times of danger.

Other adults and youngsters will help groom the infant; this is a way of making friends as

well as keeping clean. The big males will accompany mother and infant for protection, so the young baboon grows up in a close social group. Even the stern males allow it to play around them. As it grows older it will play with other youngsters. By playing they learn and practice all the skills they will need in adult life. Even now the older baboons keep an eye on the baby, rushing to its aid if needed.

Future boss of the baboons

Gradually it learns its place in the society, how to escape or protect itself from an attacker such as a leopard and how to hunt and gather food. All the time as it is growing up it is watching the adults and copying the way they do things, until this comes naturally. Finally as an adult, just like a human, it will win a special place within the group: it may even become the chief baboon one day!